Instant Prezi Starter

A user-friendly, step-by-step introductory guide to using Prezi, a web-based presentation application program ideal for engaging your audience

Dr. Minerva M. Ladores

BIRMINGHAM - MUMBAI

Instant Prezi Starter

Copyright © 2013 Packt Publishing

All rights reserved. No part of this book may be reproduced, stored in a retrieval system, or transmitted in any form or by any means, without the prior written permission of the publisher, except in the case of brief quotations embedded in critical articles or reviews.

Every effort has been made in the preparation of this book to ensure the accuracy of the information presented. However, the information contained in this book is sold without warranty, either express or implied. Neither the author, nor Packt Publishing, and its dealers and distributors will be held liable for any damages caused or alleged to be caused directly or indirectly by this book.

Packt Publishing has endeavored to provide trademark information about all of the companies and products mentioned in this book by the appropriate use of capitals. However, Packt Publishing cannot guarantee the accuracy of this information.

First published: June 2013

Production Reference: 1190613

Published by Packt Publishing Ltd.
Livery Place
35 Livery Street
Birmingham B3 2PB, UK.

ISBN 978-1-84969-702-6

www.packtpub.com

Credits

Author
Dr. Minerva M. Ladores

Acquisition Editor
Usha Iyer

Content Commissioning Editor
Neha Nagwekar

Technical Editor
Sonali S. Vernekar

Project Coordinator
Amigya Khurana

Proofreader
Paul Hindle

Graphics
Ronak Dhruv

Production Coordinator
Arvindkumar Gupta

Cover Work
Arvindkumar Gupta

Cover Work
Manu Joseph

About the Author

Dr. Minerva M. Ladores has 20 years of teaching experience in early childhood and higher education. She has taught online and face-to-face courses on instructional technology, educational foundations, early childhood education, and cultural differences – both graduate and undergraduate levels - at Frostburg State University, University of Cincinnati, and University of the Philippines. She has presented at national and international conferences on the topics of educational technology and cultural diversity. Her current interests are online learning, instructional uses of mobile devices, and integrating Web 2.0 tools (such as Prezi) in teaching.

> I would like to express my gratitude to my mom Naty, Annie, and Dave, for being there for me.
>
> Thanks to dearest John for all his wise suggestions and encouragement that kept me going (and sumptuous meals while I was working on this book!).
>
> I would also like to thank my editors (Maria and Neha) and project coordinator (Amigya) at Packt Publishing for all their assistance in the development of this book.

www.packtpub.com

Support files, eBooks, discount offers and more

You might want to visit www.packtpub.com for support files and downloads related to your book.

Did you know that Packt offers eBook versions of every book published, with PDF and ePub files available? You can upgrade to the eBook version at www.packtpub.com and as a print book customer, you are entitled to a discount on the eBook copy. Get in touch with us at service@packtpub.com for more details.

At www.packtpub.com, you can also read a collection of free technical articles, sign up for a range of free newsletters and receive exclusive discounts and offers on Packt books and eBooks.

packtlib.packtpub.com

Do you need instant solutions to your IT questions? PacktLib is Packt's online digital book library. Here, you can access, read and search across Packt's entire library of books.

Why Subscribe?

- Fully searchable across every book published by Packt
- Copy and paste, print and bookmark content
- On demand and accessible via web browser

Free Access for Packt account holders

If you have an account with Packt at www.packtpub.com, you can use this to access PacktLib today and view nine entirely free books. Simply use your login credentials for immediate access.

Table of Contents

Instant Prezi Starter — 1
- **So, what is Prezi?** — 3
- **Installation** — 5
- **Quick start – creating your first Prezi presentation** — 6
  - Step 1 – creating a new project — 6
  - Step 2 – adding text — 7
  - Step 3 – adding a symbol — 9
  - Step 4 – selecting a template — 11
  - Step 5 – adding frames — 13
  - Step 6 – adding images — 14
  - Step 7 – determining the path — 16
  - Step 8 – adding an element of surprise — 18
  - Step 9 – presenting your Prezi — 19
  - Step 10 – returning home — 20
- **Top 10 features you need to know about** — 21
  - Your Prezi library — 21
  - The Prezi online editor — 21
  - Frames and arrows — 22
  - Insert — 22
    - Diagrams — 23
    - YouTube videos — 24
    - Music — 25
    - Files — 27
    - PowerPoint presentations — 29
  - Customized themes — 31
  - The top-right menu — 34
  - Sharing options — 35
    - Invite to edit — 35
    - Start an online presentation — 36
    - Download as PDF — 37

Post-editing options for your Prezi	38
Edit Prezi	38
Present online	38
Download	39
Save a copy	40
Share	40
Privacy settings	41
Deleting your Prezi	42
People and places you should get to know	**43**
Presentation tips	43
Awesome Prezi examples	43
Prezi company resources	44
Copyright concerns	44
About Packt Publishing	45
Writing for Packt	45

Instant Prezi Starter

Welcome to *Instant Prezi Starter*. This book has been especially created to provide you with all the information that you need to get started with Prezi. You will learn the basics of Prezi, get started with building your first presentation, and discover some tips and tricks for using Prezi.

This book contains the following sections:

So, what is Prezi? section will help you find out what Prezi actually is, what you can do with it, and why it is so great.

Installation section will help you learn how to create an account on Prezi and get started fast.

Quick start – creating your first Prezi presentation section will show you a step-by-step guide on creating your first Prezi presentation.

Top 10 features you need to know about section explores Prezi features that can help you make your presentation more powerful and impressive. You will learn how to use the Prezi online editor and templates. You will also learn how to insert diagrams, graphic elements, images, and multimedia. The section will end with options for saving, sharing, and presenting your Prezi.

People and places you should get to know section provides you with many useful links to learn more about Prezi and to see great presentation examples.

So, what is Prezi?

Prezi is a web-based presentation tool. It has awesome features you can use to create compelling, attention-grabbing, and memorable presentations. We will get to the cool features later. First, let me talk about it being a web-based presentation tool. By "web-based," I mean that you create your presentations online using this application program. You create presentations online, present it from the web, and have a link through which your audience can access it later. You can also use Prezi as a collaboration tool by sharing your Prezi and allowing members of your group to edit the presentation with you in real time. During a Prezi meeting, up to 10 members of your group can make changes on a Prezi as you brainstorm your ideas or discuss your points. So, while it is largely a presentation tool, Prezi can also function as a tool for brainstorming and discussion. This is possible because of the way Prezi has been laid out and the various flowcharts you can build to illustrate your points. In this sense, Prezi also functions as a mind mapping tool.

So, Prezi is an online presentation tool that you can also use for brainstorming, mind mapping, and real-time collaboration. It comes with features that you can harness to create highly visual and engaging presentations.

Now, there are several presentation tools online, but Prezi is different. Working with most slideshow presentations is like working with a stack of index cards or poster boards. We add text and illustrations on each card, then we present our cards one at a time.

First you view the first slide, then the second, and so on, as shown in the following diagram:

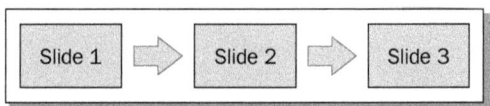

In slideshow presentations, information is presented one slide at a time

Similar to slideshow presentation tools, you use Prezi to present your ideas by adding text and illustrations on a given space. What makes Prezi awesome, however, are the panning and zooming features you should use to make a greater impact on your audience.

When it comes to making a presentation using Prezi, imagine yourself in front of a huge white board the size of a wall. You begin by typing text and illustrations on this board. In Prezi, this is referred to as the **canvas**.

It is like having an exhibit, but you would want to guide your viewers' eyes through the texts and illustrations you have placed on your canvas. Which one should they look at first? Next? So, you add numbers to each item. This will be the path your viewers' eyes would take as they travel from one element to another, as shown in the following diagram:

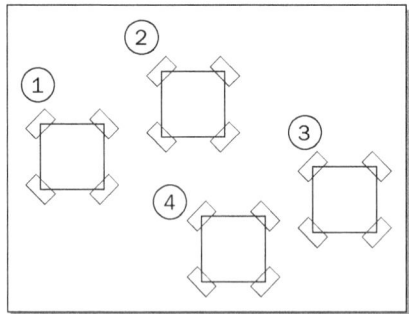

In Prezi, you guide your viewer's eyes by adding a numbered path

Now imagine you have a video camera. Imagine viewing your whiteboard and focusing on the first item, then moving the video (without turning it off) to view the second item. In Prezi, a similar panning movement occurs as you move from one frame to the next following the path you have indicated, as shown in the following diagram:

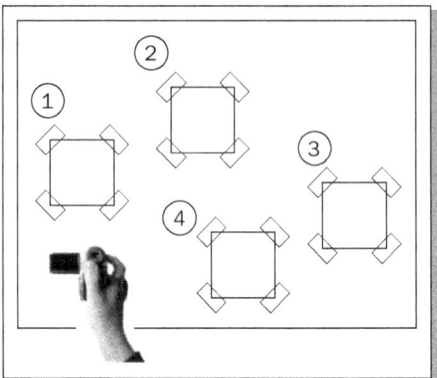

A Prezi presentation is like viewing your presentation through a video camera, as it pans across the canvas and zooming into focus points at certain times

This sense of movement created by panning makes the presentation eye-catching. The motion produced helps to keep your viewer's attention as you move from one item on your presentation to the next. Imagine if, given the preceding diagram, we pan 1-2-4-3 instead of 1-2-3-4. Can you imagine how different that would be? Or how about if we were to place the elements in a straight row? Will it be as attractive? Think of the many different ways you can be creative with this Prezi feature!

Installation

Prezi is a web-based tool, and it is best to work on it online. You can get started in four easy steps as follows:

1. Go to `http://prezi.com/`.
2. Click on **Sign Up Now** located in the middle of the screen, or **Sign Up** located in the upper right-hand corner.
3. Choose one of the following options for a Prezi license:
    - **Public**: This is free. You will have 100 MB of storage, which is enough for a few presentations. You can edit and share the Prezi presentations you create. Your presentations will be public.
    - **Enjoy**: For a fee, you will have 500 MB of storage. On top of that, you have the option to make your presentations private and use your own logo. Subscribers also get premium customer support where you can get answers within one day.
    - **Pro**: If you upgrade to a Pro license, you'll get 2 GB of storage. In addition to having the option to have private presentations and using your own logo, you will also be able to download Prezi Desktop. You use Prezi Desktop to work offline securely.
    - **Student and Teacher Licenses**: You can register for an Enjoy Edu license for free if your school has an official website. Use a school e-mail account when signing up. You can create private presentations, use your own logo, and have 500 MB of storage space. If you want the ability to work offline or need more space, you can upgrade to a Pro Edu license for a fee.

    Decide which option is most appropriate for you and then click on the button that says **Try Now**. Follow the prompts for signing up. You will be asked for your name, e-mail address, and a password. It may be a good idea for you to write down the e-mail and password you used before you forget. You should also check the box signifying that you agree to Prezi's terms of use.

    If you have a Facebook account, you might like to log in using your Facebook account information. Just click on **Log in with Facebook**.

4. Once you have signed up, you can log in and use Prezi any time you wish by going to `http://prezi.com/` and putting in your e-mail address and password.

    And that's it! Now you're ready to create your first Prezi!

Instant Prezi Starter

Quick start – creating your first Prezi presentation

Prezi is a presentation tool. You use it to create presentations with text and images you wish to share with an audience. In this first project, you will learn how to create a new Prezi project, add text, add a symbol, change the overall look by changing the theme, add a frame, add an image, determine the path, toggle between presentation and edit modes, and use the home button.

Step 1 – creating a new project

To create a new project, you must first log in to your Prezi account and launch the Prezi editor.

1. Go to http://prezi.com/ and log in. The login button is in the upper right-hand corner of your screen. Enter your e-mail address and password. Click on the blue button **Log In**.
2. A new window will open showing your account. Click on the blue button **New Prezi**, the Prezi application will be launched. Give it a few seconds.
3. You will see a window with templates to choose from. Scroll down and select **Start from blank** and click on **Start blank prezi**.
4. You will find yourself on the edit window of Prezi, which should look like the following screenshot:

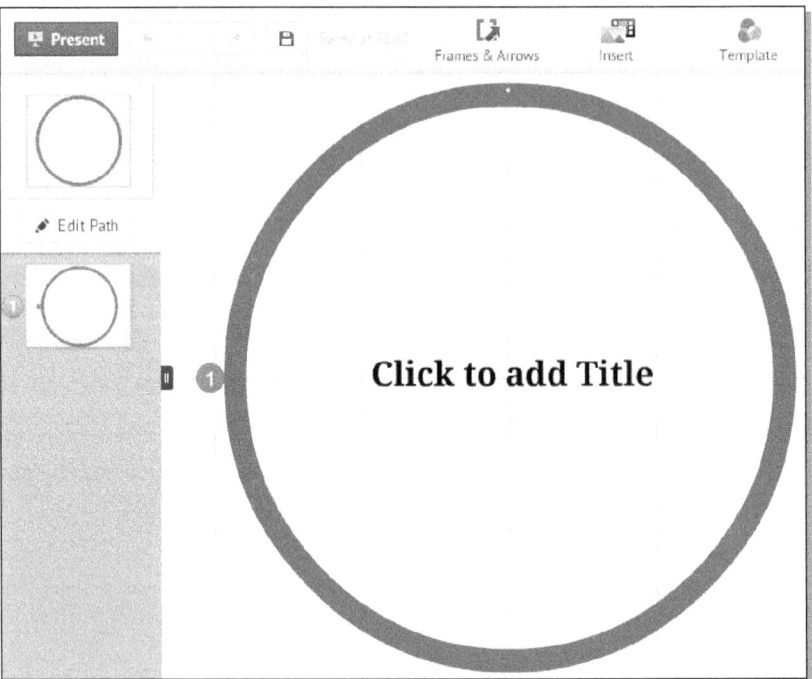

Step 2 – adding text

Most presentations require text. It is easy to add, edit, format, and move text elements in Prezi.

1. Click on the area where it says **Click to add text**. A text box with a blinking cursor will appear as shown in the following screenshot:

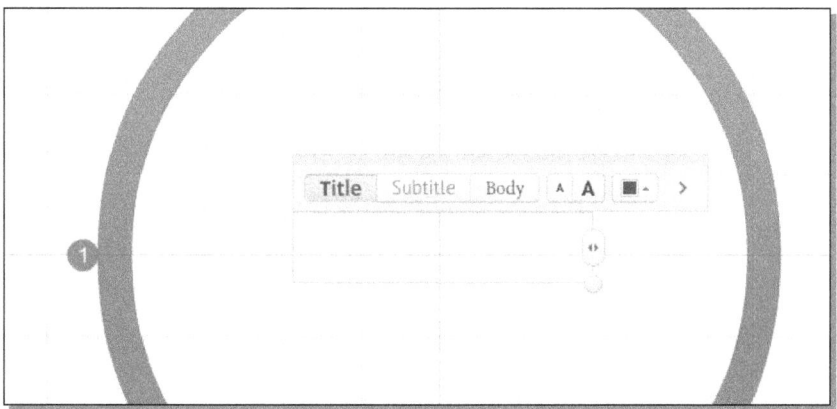

2. Start typing `Which do you think is the key to success?` You might like to break the sentence and hit the *Enter* key between the words, as shown in the following screenshot:

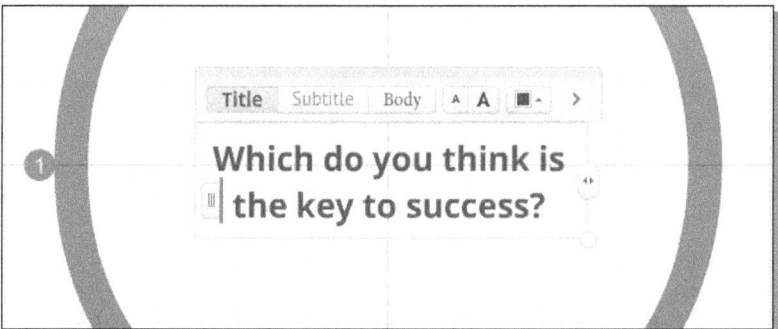

3. When you have finished typing, click on the outside of the circle. This will signify that you have finished typing within this textbox. This is now a text element on your presentation. Click on this text element and you should see a blue line surrounding your text as shown in the following screenshot:

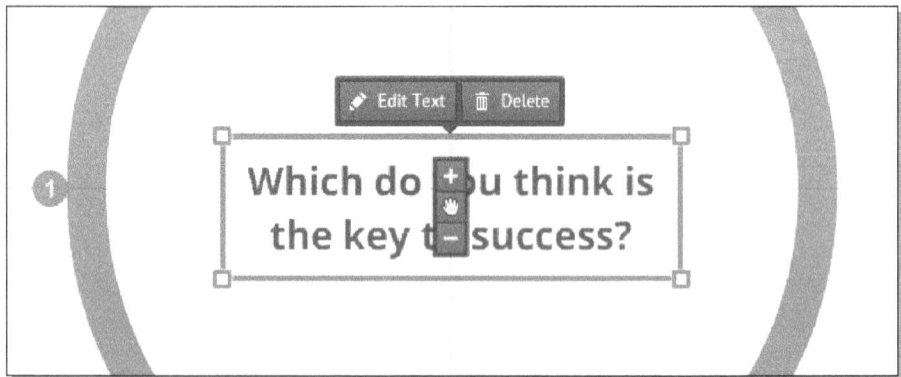

4. If you click on **Edit Text**, you will be able to make changes on what you have typed in the text box. If you want to get rid of this text element, you can click on the trash can to **Delete**. To change the size of the text, click on the (+) or (-) signs. Try it! Click on the (+) three times, then click on the (-) three times. See what happens. Then, click and hold on the hand icon to move the text element. I'd like you to move it higher inside the circular frame. The page will look like the following screenshot:

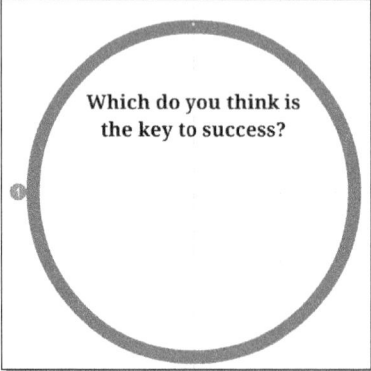

5. Now let us add more text inside the frame. In Prezi, you can click anywhere to add text. Click on a spot within the circular frame and type the word `passion`. While in text typing mode, select **Subtitle**. This will change your font style. Click on a different spot and write the word `talent`. Click on various other spots to add `hardwork`, `persistence`, and other words you think are a key to success, as shown in the following screenshot:

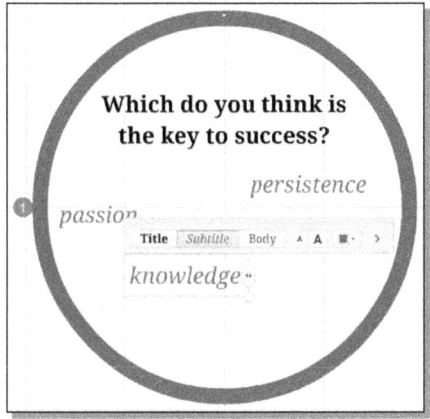

You've just added text elements in your presentation! Congratulations!

Step 3 – adding a symbol

Now it's time to add visual elements to your presentation. Graphic images help the audience understand your message better. Prezi comes with symbols you can add to illustrate your ideas.

1. Look at the top of your screen and locate the three editing tools. Click on the **Insert** button.

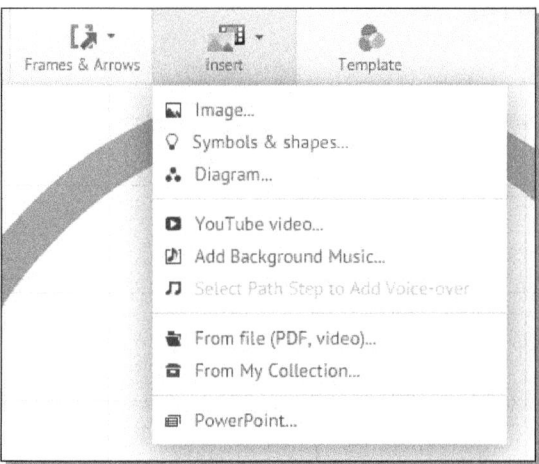

Instant Prezi Starter

2. Click on **Symbols & shapes...**. The **Styles** option will show on the right side of the screen. Click on **Simple Dark**. Scroll down and look for an image of a key. Double-click on the key to insert. The option will look like the following screenshot:

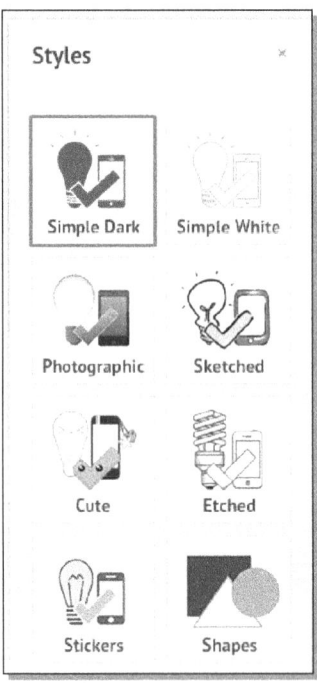

3. The key symbol will now be inserted within your circular frame. Click on it to rotate and move it to a better location within the frame as shown in the following screenshot:

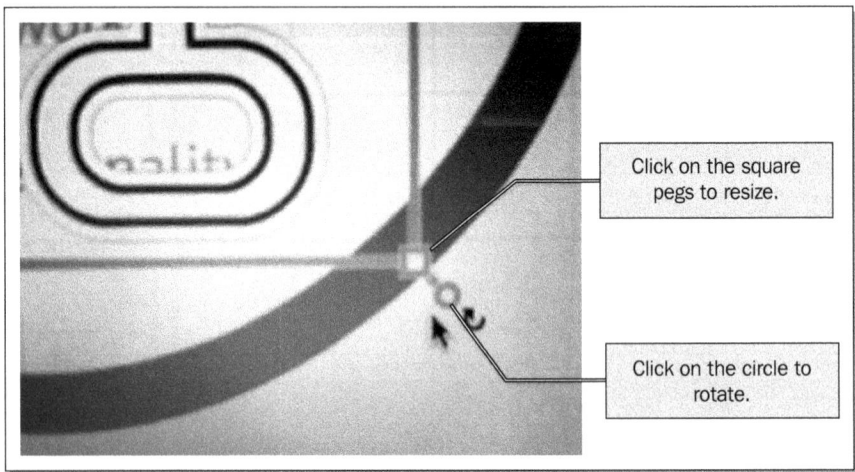

4. Play with the main question and the words on your frame. Resize the question and make it bigger. Rotate the words. Relocate until you're satisfied with the layout. I came out with something like the following screenshot:

Step 4 – selecting a template

Templates can change the overall appearance of your presentation instantly. You can click on the different templates and select the best one that matches your message.

1. Look at the top of your screen and locate the three editing tools. Click on the **Template** button. Select a theme that you like.
2. Click on one theme at a time and observe as your presentation changes font styles and colors. Give it a few seconds for the changes to occur.

Instant Prezi Starter

3. Once you've come across the theme you prefer, click on the **Template** button once more to toggle out of it and for the menu to disappear. The menu will look like the following screenshot:

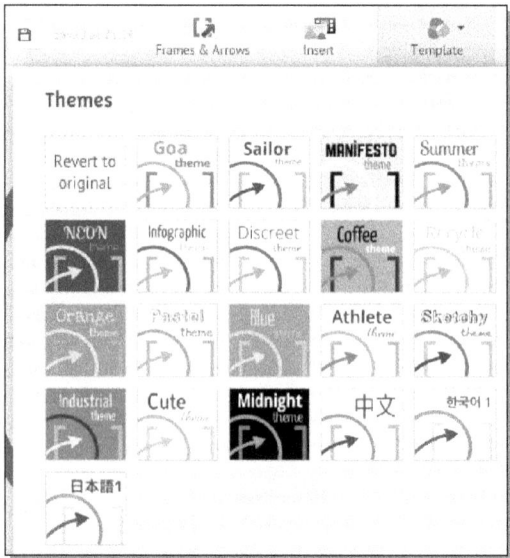

The following screenshot displays our first Prezi project using the Pastel theme:

Step 5 – adding frames

In Prezi, items you want to show together should be placed within a frame. So far, we have one circular frame with a question, a symbol, and a few words. You can add more frames to your presentation.

1. Add a new frame by clicking on the **Frames & Arrows** icon on the edit menu. Then, click on **+ Add Frame** from the drop-down menu. A rectangular frame should appear next to our first circular frame as shown in the following screenshot:

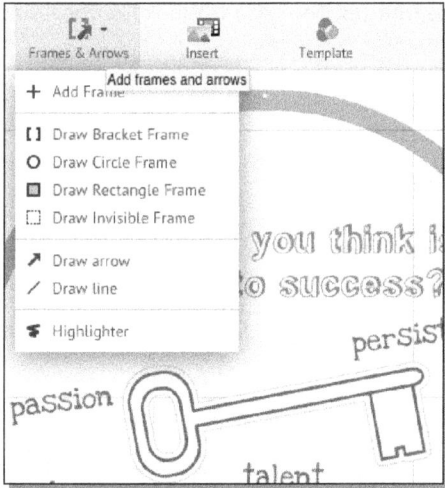

2. Click on **Click to add text** and write `To unlock success, you need many keys!` as shown in the following screenshot:

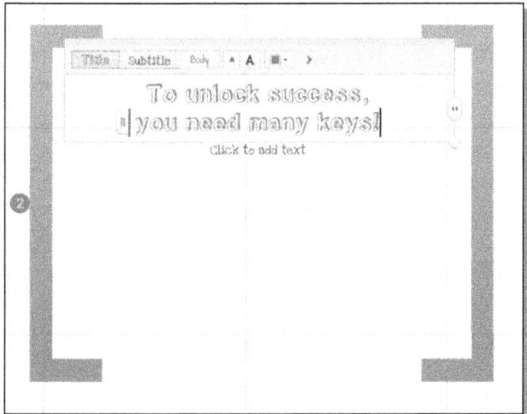

There you have it, a new frame! For your future projects, there are other options you can choose from: bracket, circle, rectangle, and invisible.

Instant Prezi Starter

Step 6 – adding images

Presentations are more meaningful when images are available. Images that illustrate the text help viewers comprehend the message.

1. Add an image on the second frame by clicking on the **Insert** icon from the edit menu and select **Image**. You can choose to add an image from your own collection or directly from Google. To add an image from your own collection, click on **From your computer** then search your hard drive for the appropriate image. Using your own images for your own presentations is the best thing to do in terms of copyright compliance. The other option is to select **From Google Images**. The page will look like the following screenshot:

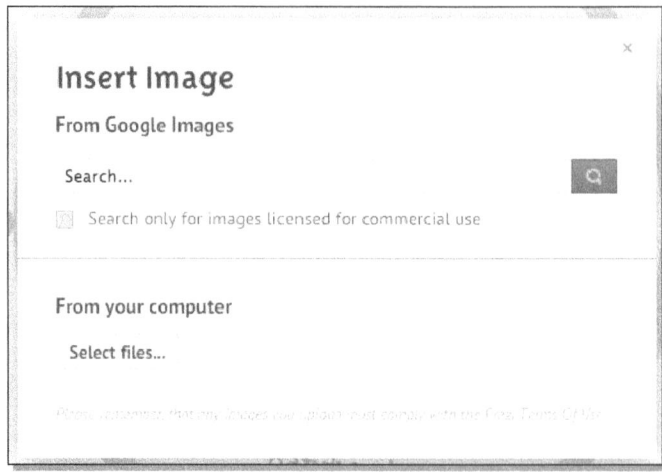

2. You can easily insert images directly from Google. This feature makes it very easy to create a Prezi presentation fast! Click on **From Google Images**; a search box will appear. Type `locks` and click on the blue magnifying glass search icon. Depending on the project you are creating, you may want to put a check mark on **Search only for images licensed for commercial use**. Again, this is to address copyright concerns. However, doing so limits the choices you have in terms of images. If you keep this unchecked, you will find more options. Copyright compliance is your responsibility, so be mindful of when and which images to use. The page will look like the following screenshot:

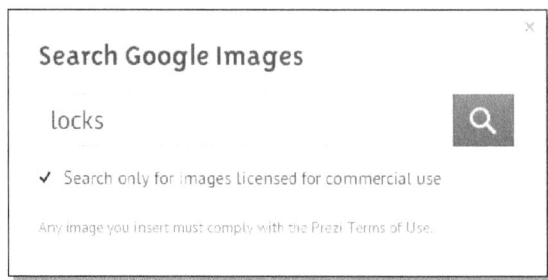

3. Several options will show. Select the one you think is most appropriate for our message. The screen will look like the following while you are still searching for an image to use. Once you find an appropriate image, click on it and then click on the button labeled **Insert**:

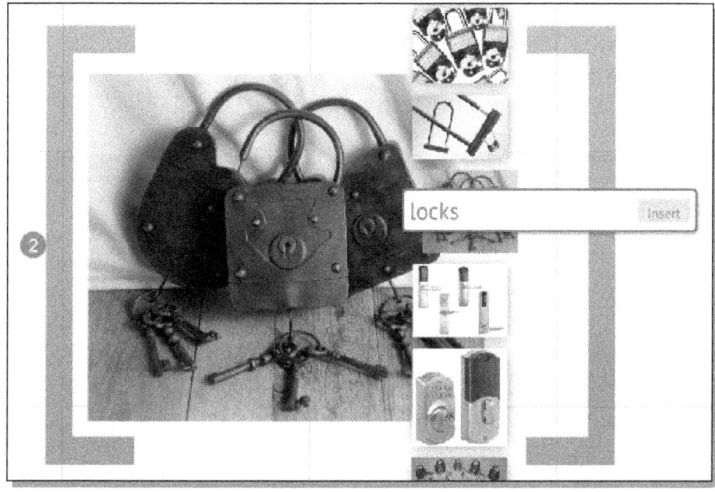

4. Give a few seconds for the image to be processed and inserted in your frame. Once it has been inserted, resize and relocate it to a better position. You've just learned how to add an image! The page will look like the following screenshot:

Step 7 – determining the path

Now let us talk about the path. Notice that there are numbers right before each frame. Remember the video camera analogy? The numbers will be the path your presentation will take. This means the view will begin with the first circular frame then move towards the second bracket frame. The series of frames as it will be viewed is shown on the left-hand side of the screen. If you're familiar with slideshows, the left-hand side is very similar to the series of slides you see while working on a slideshow presentation. In Prezi, these are referred to as frames. The page will look like the following screenshot:

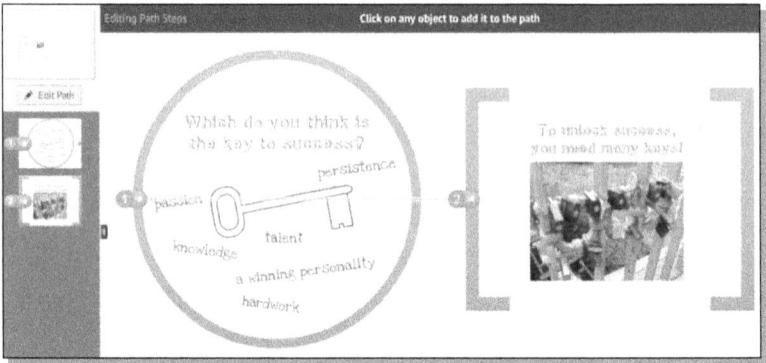

1. Click on **Edit Path**. The numbers and lines connecting them will show.
2. Click on the image of padlocks you have inserted. A third frame, the image of the padlocks alone, will be added to the list of frames. You will see this new frame on the left-hand side of the screen. You should now see three frames as shown in the following screenshot:

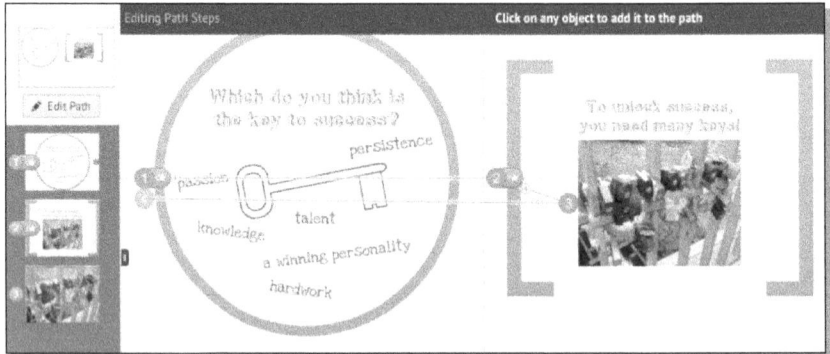

3. What if you want to add a frame between two existing frames? That will be easy! Look closely on the path numbers and you should see a tiny plus sign. Click on the tiny plus sign right after path number 1. Click on it, and without letting go, drag it towards the key symbol. Once you see the key symbol being highlighted, let go. Now you have inserted a new frame! Check the sequence on your left to see what frames you have so far. The page will look like the following screenshot:

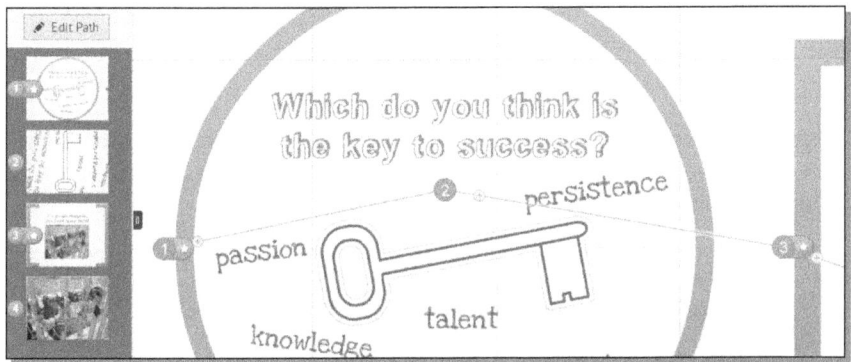

4. Now if you change your mind and wish to delete a path point, while still on **Edit Path**, click on the frame you want to delete. You will see a red cross mark in the upper right-hand corner of the frame. Click on the red cross mark to delete as shown in the following screenshot:

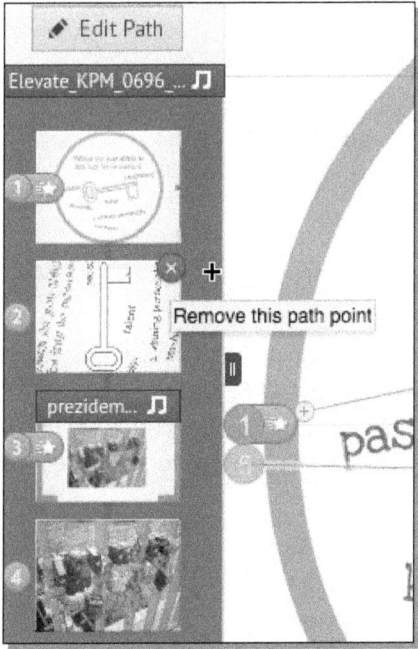

Instant Prezi Starter

    Another way to delete a path point is to click on the path number and pull it away to an empty spot and let go. Like a rubber band, you will see the connecting lines bounce back and the path point will have been deleted.

5. Click on **Edit Path** again to return to editing.

Step 8 – adding an element of surprise

Be creative in Prezi by hiding a text element and then zooming towards it.

1. Go to the image of the padlocks.
2. Select one padlock towards the middle of the picture and type the sentence `Go for it!` Resize the sentence so it fits inside the padlock. Rotate it so that it aligns with the padlock as shown in the following screenshot:

3. Click on **Edit Path** and add a path point to this sentence. This becomes the last frame. Click on **Edit Path** again to toggle out.
4. Click on **Present** and voila! Watch as you end the presentation with a dramatic twisting and zooming motion from the image of padlocks diving in towards `Go for it!`.

Instant Prezi Starter

In this project, we hid words within an image. There are other ways you can add an element of surprise. You can hide an image inside a word or hide words inside a word. You may want to write an important quotation in a small font size so it doesn't show at the beginning of your presentation and then zoom in to it towards the end, leaving your audience with an important message to think about. Take advantage of this Prezi feature and make your presentation unforgettable!

Step 9 – presenting your Prezi

Your Prezi is now ready to be presented! You can toggle between presentation and edit modes.

1. Click on the blue **Present** button located in the uppermost left-hand corner of the screen. Doing so will take you to the presentation mode, which is automatically in full screen. Use this mode when you want to present your Prezi, as shown in the following screenshot:

2. You will be asked if you will allow full screen with keyboard controls. Click on **Allow** as shown in the following screenshot:

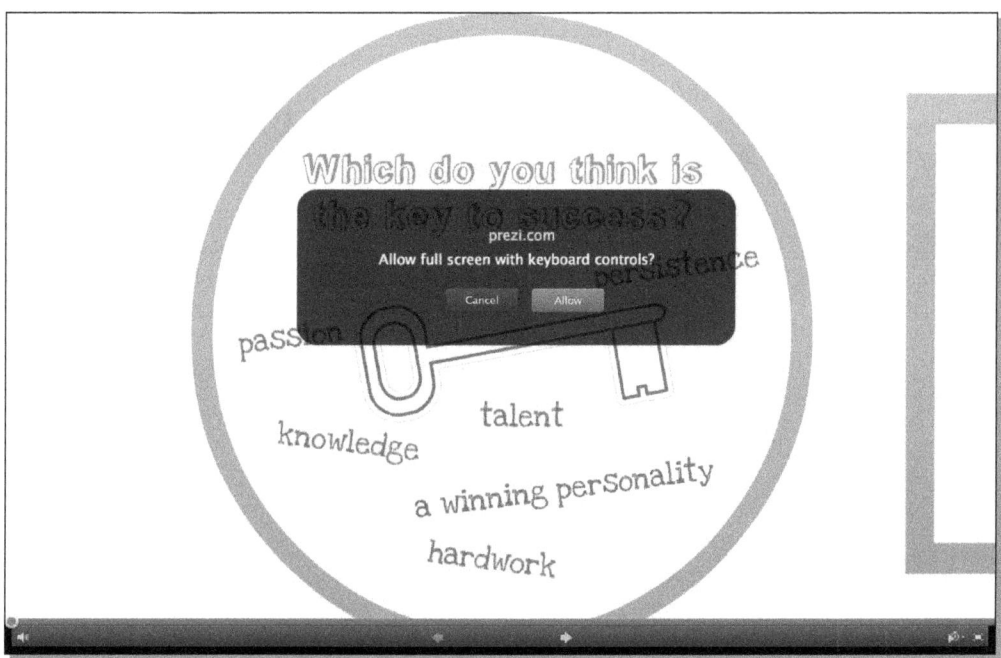

While you're in presentation mode, click on the left and right arrows located at the bottom of the screen to move from one frame to another.

3. If you want to exit full screen, click on the *Esc* key on your computer keyboard. This will take you back to edit mode.

   You can present your Prezi offline by downloading your presentation as a portable Prezi. Instructions on how to do this are provided in the *Top 10 features you need to know about* section.

Step 10 – returning home

Prezi has a huge canvas you can get lost in. If you are in edit mode and accidentally veered off the area where your items are located, you'll find yourself facing a blank screen and wondering, where did they all go? Hover your cursor towards the right-hand side of your screen and the home button will appear as shown in the following screenshot:

Clicking on the home button will take you back to the overview of everything you have placed on your canvas up to that point. So, whenever you get lost on your canvas, remember to click on home!

You've just finished your first Prezi project! You've learned how to add text on your canvas, add a symbol, change the theme, add an image, resize and relocate objects, add a frame, edit the path, add an element of surprise, and toggle between presentation and edit modes. Congratulations!

Instant Prezi Starter

Top 10 features you need to know about

Let's take a closer look at the Prezi online editor and the various tools available to you.

Your Prezi library

Go to `http://www.prezi.com` and log in to your Prezi account. You should see your first project in your Prezi library. The Prezi library will contain all the presentations you create in Prezi. In the following example, you can see that I have 35 prezis. At this point, you should have at least one; your first project. Click on your first Prezi project then click on **EDIT** to launch the Prezi online editor:

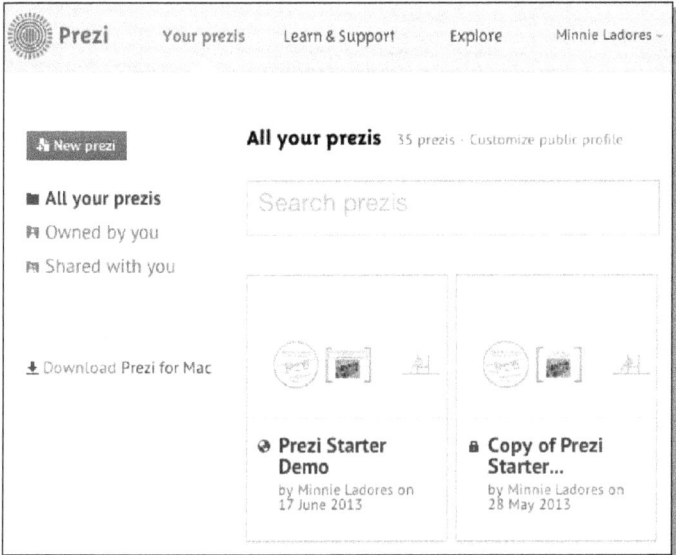

The Prezi online editor

Look at the editing tools located on the top menu of your screen. There are 3 icons: **Frames & Arrows**, **Insert**, and **Template**.

Frames and arrows

Click on **Frames & Arrows** and then look at the choices in the drop-down menu. Clicking on the first one, **+ Add Frames**, adds a bracket frame on your canvas. The other options are: **Draw Bracket Frame**, **Draw Circle Frame**, **Draw Rectangular Frame**, and **Draw Invisible Frame**. Use frames to group elements connected to an idea you are presenting. Sometimes, visible frames add an element of interest. Other times, you may find a frame to be distracting, and using an invisible frame may be the better option. The page will look like the following screenshot:

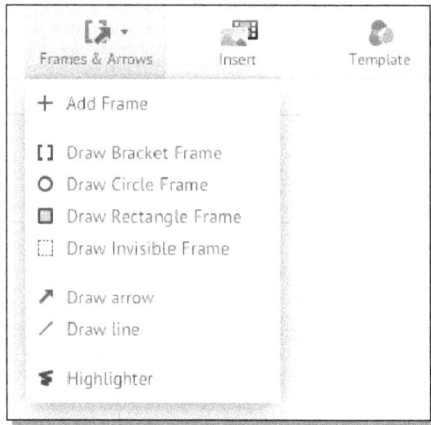

Arrows, lines, and the highlighter are tools you can use to help focus attention on a word or an image. Click on **Draw arrow**, **Draw line**, or **Highlighter** to use any of these tools.

Insert

Prezi makes it easy for you to insert items into your presentation. You can insert images, symbols and shapes, diagrams, YouTube videos, music, files, and pre-existing PowerPoint slides. The page will look like the following screenshot:

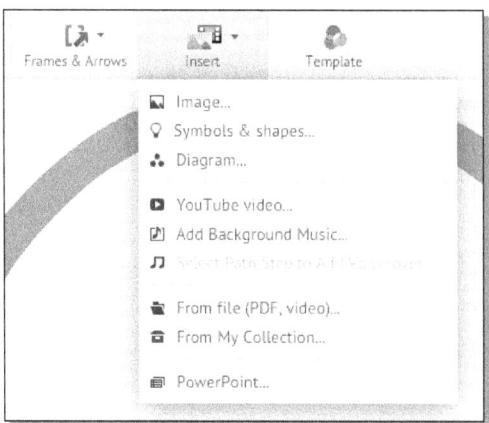

Diagrams

The third item on the **Insert** drop-down menu is **Diagram...** as shown in the following screenshot:

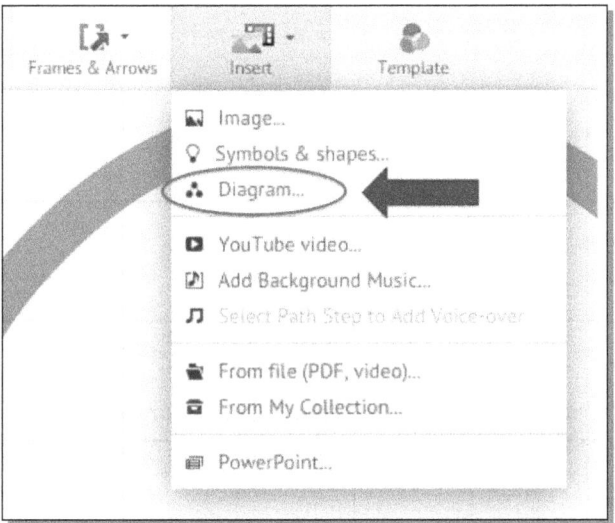

Click on **Diagram...** and study the different options from the window that pops up. The page will look like the following screenshot:

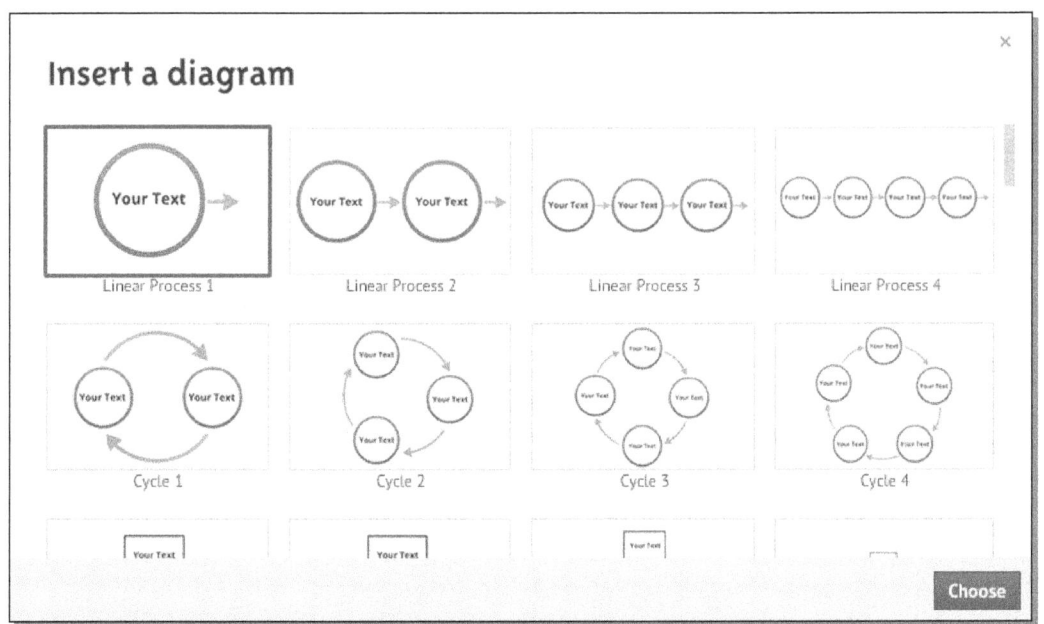

Instant Prezi Starter

Diagrams are most useful for showing relationships between ideas. A diagram may have two or more frames. Scroll down to see more options. Look for the **Iceberg** as shown in the following screenshot:

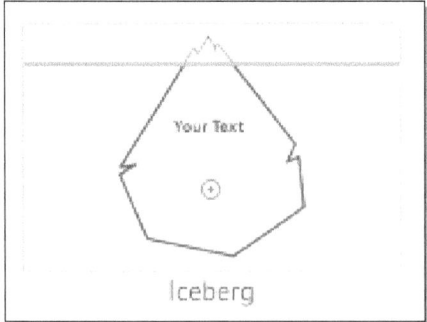

The Iceberg is great for illustrating your point if you mean to show what the tip of an issue may seem to be and the bigger issue that may be hidden. Look at the other diagrams that are available that you can use to present your ideas visually.

YouTube videos

The fourth item on the **Insert** drop-down menu is **YouTube video...**. Prezi makes it easy to insert a video in your presentation. These videos will play automatically within your presentation. To insert a video, first look for a YouTube video you want to insert on a different browser window. Copy the web address of this video. Then, return to Prezi. While on edit mode, click on **Insert**. Select **YouTube video...** as shown in the following screenshot:

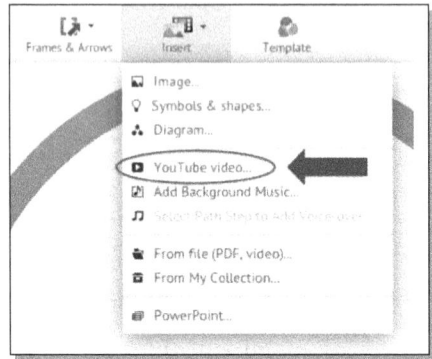

A window will pop up. Paste the YouTube link in the textbox and hit **Insert** as shown in the following screenshot:

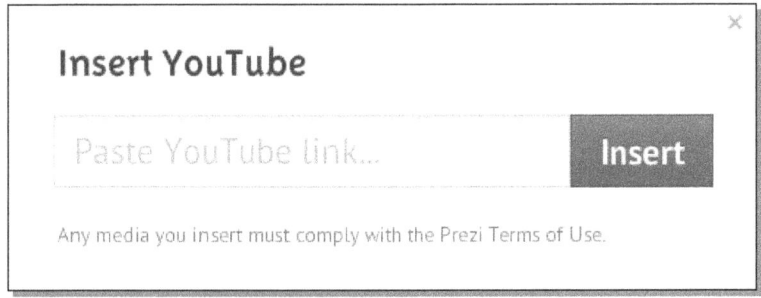

Give it a few seconds to load. Remember to place your video within a frame or to add a path to it so it will play during your presentation. The video will play automatically once you reach the frame or path in which the video is located. It will be a good idea, however, to go through your whole Prezi at least ten minutes before your presentation so that your videos will have time to download. This way, your video will play seamlessly when you present. Then sit back, relax, and watch!

Music

The fifth item on the **Insert** drop-down menu is **Add Background Music...**. Adding background music can enhance your presentation, especially if you plan on making the Prezi available for an audience to view at their convenience. If you want to add music, click on **Insert** and select **Add Background Music...** as shown in the following screenshot:

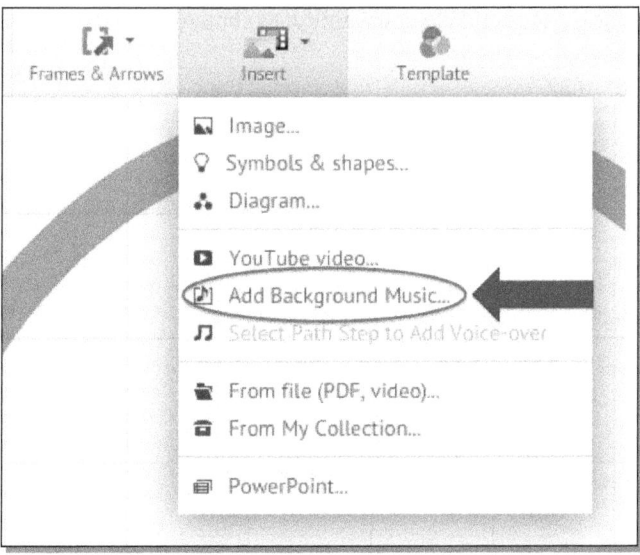

Instant Prezi Starter

A window will pop up showing files on your hard drive. Select the song or sound file you wish to add as shown in the following screenshot:

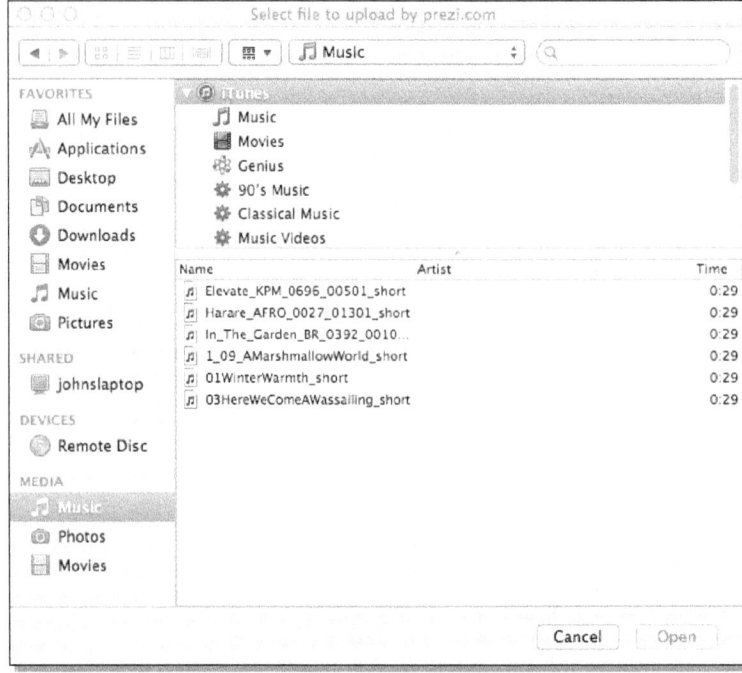

Once you have selected a file, give it a few seconds to load. You should see the music file being loaded right below the **Edit Path** button. Click on the play button to listen. Click on **Done** once you're satisfied that this is the sound file you wanted, as shown in the following screenshot:

If you picked the wrong file or changed your mind, go to your editing tools and click on **Insert**. Select **Replace Background Music...** and locate the right file from your hard drive.

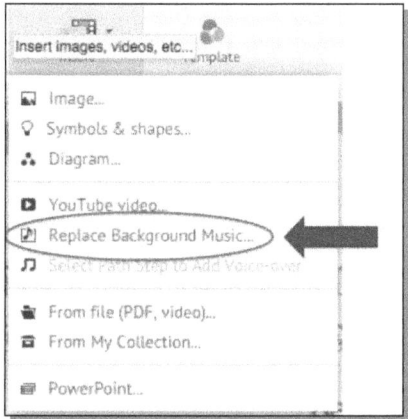

Once you are satisfied with the sound file you have selected, click on **Present** and see how it works!

Files

The seventh item on the **Insert** drop-down menu is **From file (PDF, video)...**. There are times when you may want to show a document during your presentation. Perhaps it is a form that the audience needs to be familiar with, or it could be a work sample that you want to show. In any case, you can upload documents in many different formats including a portable document file (PDF), videos (`.mov`, `.m4v`), and images (`.jpg`, `.tiff`). To add a file from your hard drive, click on **Insert** then select **From file (PDF, video)...** as shown in the following screenshot:

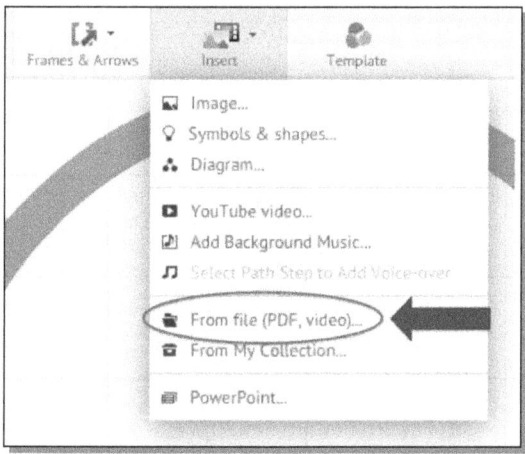

Locate the file you wish to embed in your presentation. Once you have selected the correct file, allow a few seconds for it to load. You should see a grey window with the word **Processing** as shown in the following screenshot:

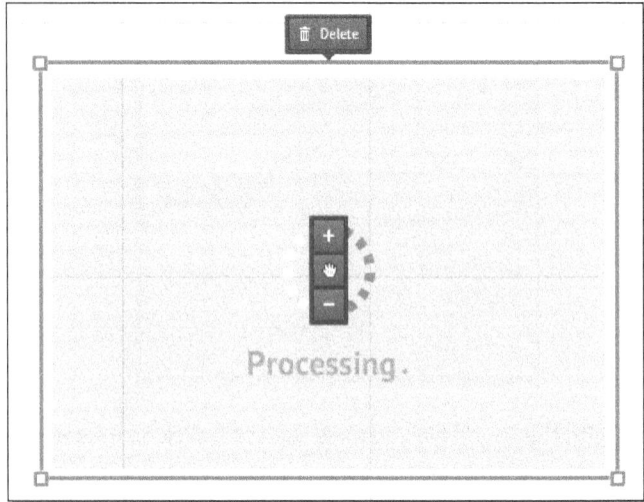

You will soon find the document embedded in your presentation. The document is shown as an image within the Prezi.

To crop, relocate, resize, or delete this image, click on the image to access the edit tools. The page will look like the following screenshot:

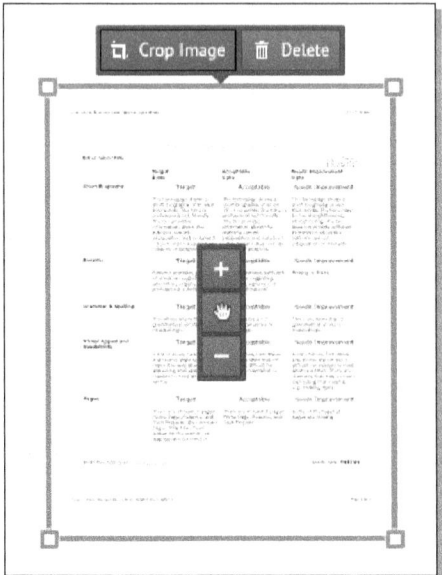

PowerPoint presentations

What if you have already created a PowerPoint presentation and you don't want to start from scratch? With Prezi, you have the option to upload a presentation you have previously created. Simply click on the last item on the **Insert** menu, which is **PowerPoint...**, as shown in the following screenshot:

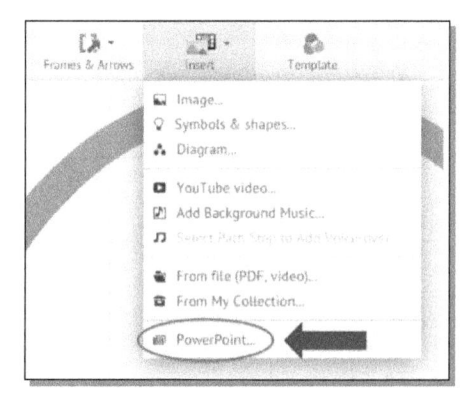

Locate the specific presentation from your hard drive. Give it a few minutes to process. You should see the contents in your slides appear on the right-hand side of your screen as shown in the following screenshot:

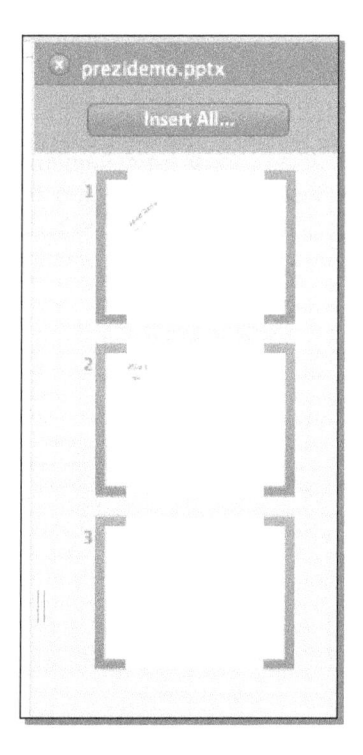

Instant Prezi Starter

Notice that the text elements have been uploaded, but not the PowerPoint theme or layout. The theme or layout that will be followed will be the one you have chosen for your Prezi. Once uploaded, you can insert selected slides or **Insert All...**. Click on **Insert All...**. Once you click, you'll see a window of suggestions for laying out your slides as shown in the following screenshot:

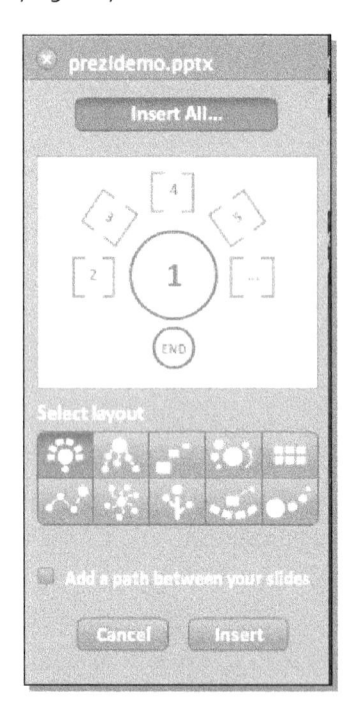

You will have several options of layouts to choose from. Remember to check **Add a path between your slides**. Then, click on **Insert**. You'll see a temporary layout on your canvas. If this is as you want it to be, click on the check mark. Otherwise, click on the **x** mark and start over. After the slides have been embedded, edit the path to your satisfaction. The page will look like the following screenshot:

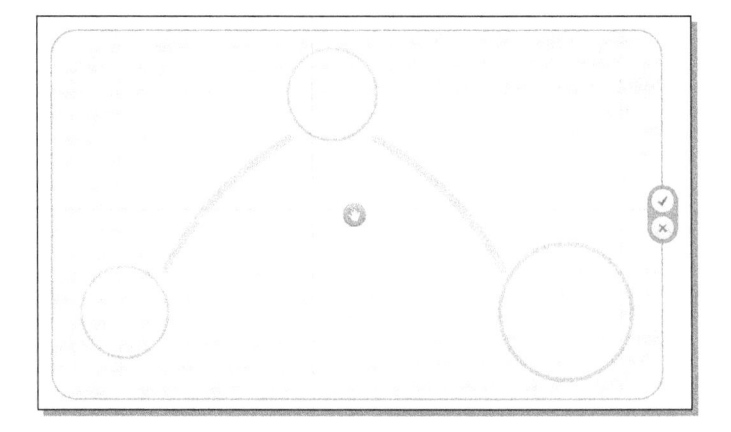

Customized themes

Now let us go to the third editing tool: **Template**. When you click on **Template**, a window of options will pop up with Themes. You are already familiar with Themes. This time, click on **Customize Current Theme...**. The theme wizard will look like the following screenshot:

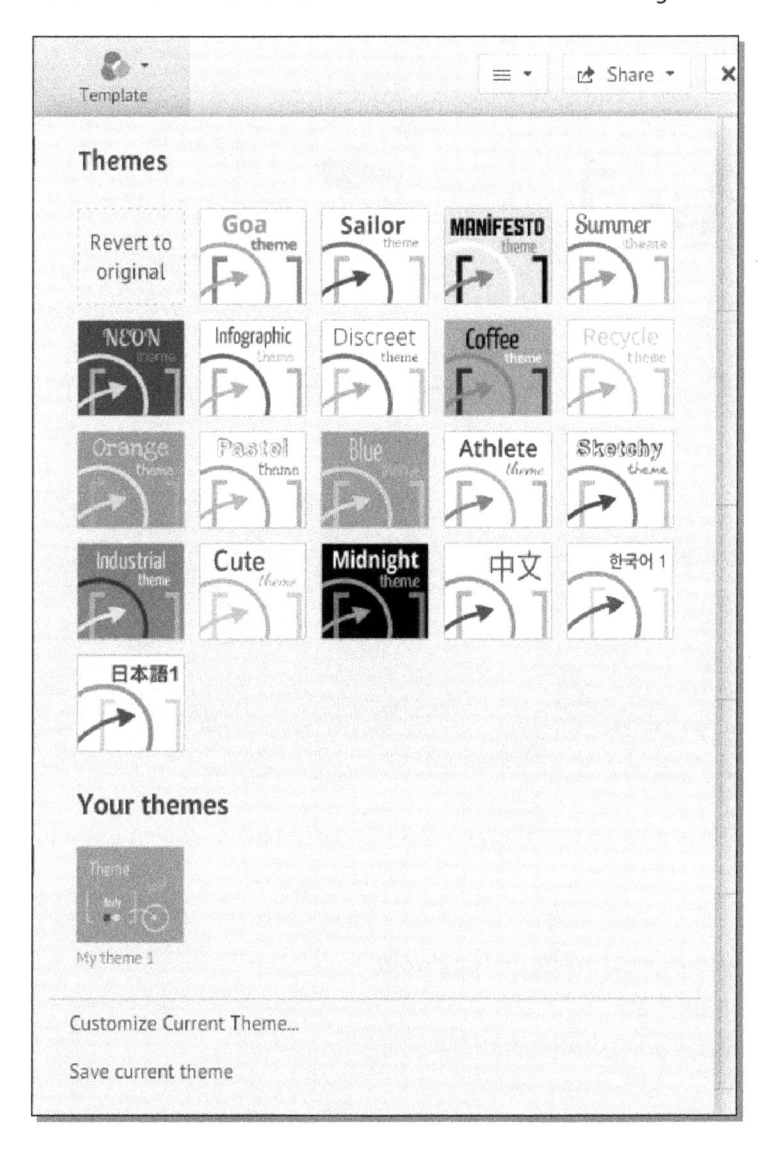

You can customize the look of your presentation using the **Theme Wizard**. The first item you can change is the background color. Select the color you prefer from the color palette. Click on Next to access the options for changing font styles and color. Click on **Next** again to access the options for changing the color of frames, arrows, and lines. Once you are satisfied, click on **Done**. The page will look like the following screenshot:

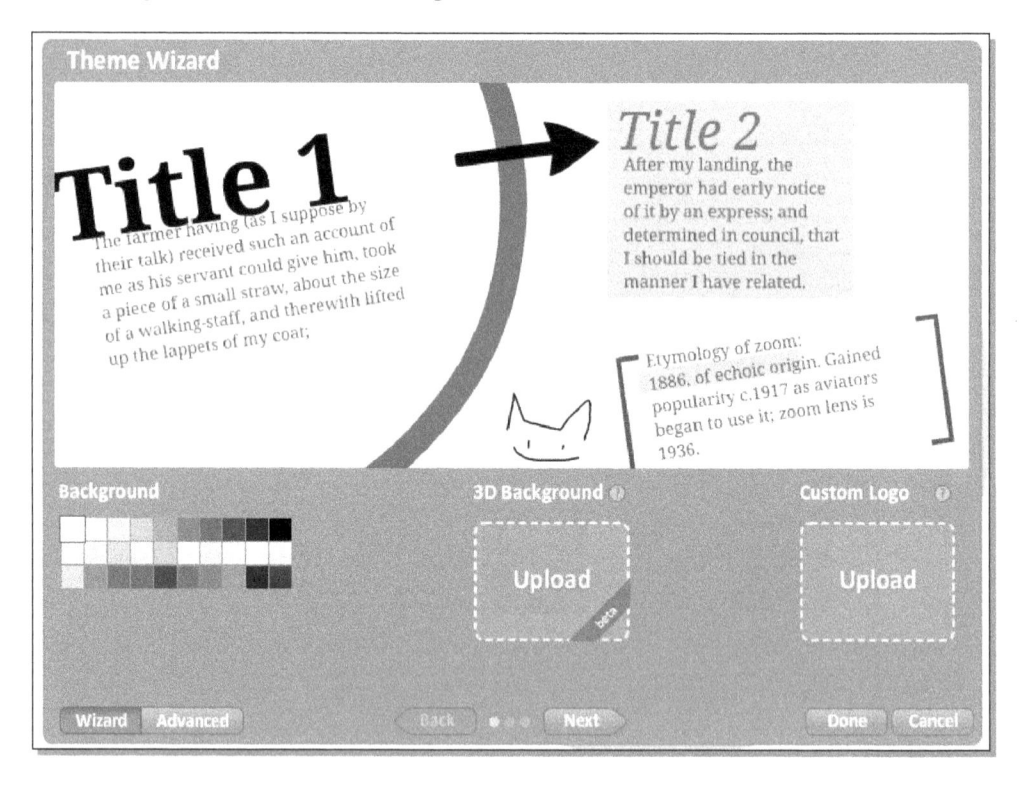

Now it's time to create your second Prezi project using a template! Implement the following steps:

1. Go to http://prezi.com.
2. Log on with your username and password.
3. Click on **New Prezi**.

Instant Prezi Starter

4. Select one template from the options given. Try **Reach the Goal,** or any other template you like, as shown in the following screenshot:

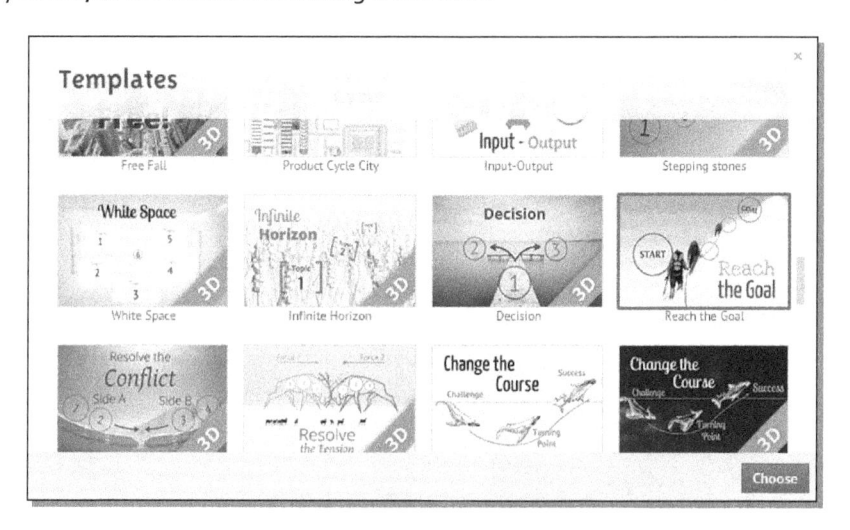

5. Wait for Prezi Editor to launch as shown in the following screenshot:

Instant Prezi Starter

6. Start editing your new Prezi. The page will look like the following screenshot:

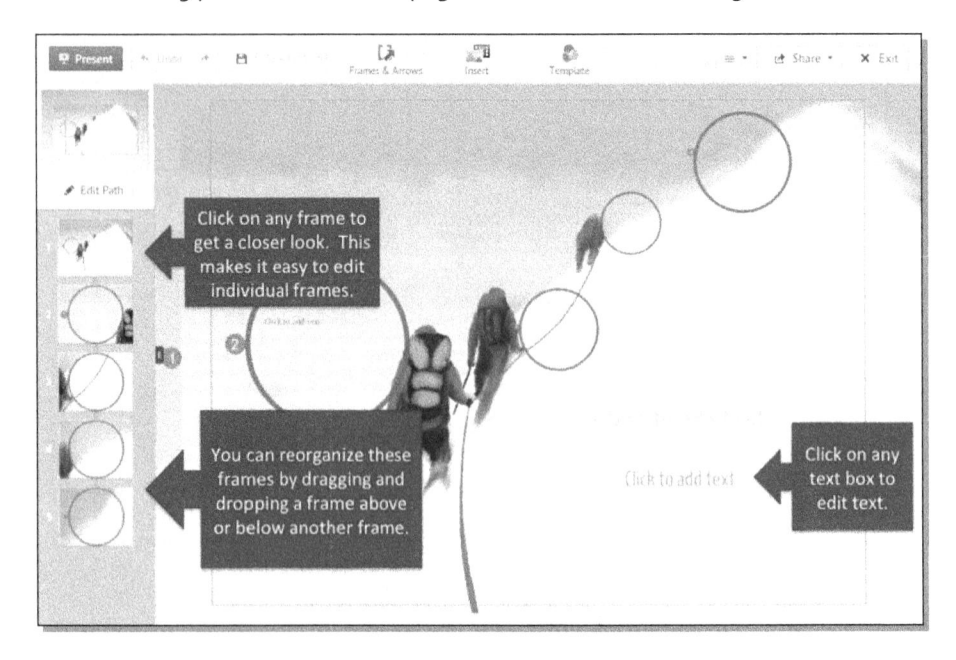

7. When you're done, click on **Exit**.

The top-right menu

Before we leave the Prezi online editor, look over at the top-right menu. There are three buttons you may wish to be familiar with: a list, **Share**, and **Exit**. Click on the list button to find all sorts of support materials such as a manual and video tutorials, as shown in the following screenshot:

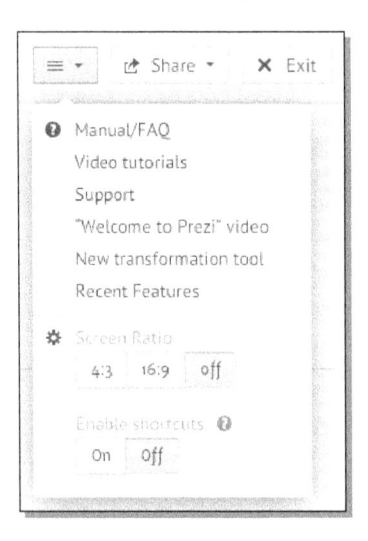

The last button is **Exit**. Click on this whenever you are done editing your work.

The middle button, **Share**, leads to more awesome Prezi features as shown in the following screenshot:

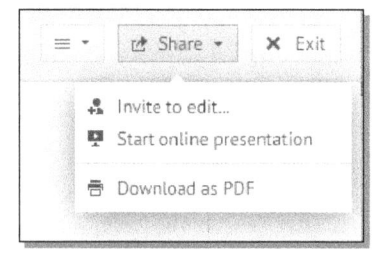

Sharing options

From the top-right menu, clicking on **Share** will give you several options for sharing your presentation with others. You can invite others to edit your presentation, start an online presentation, and download a copy of your presentation that you can use if you want to present offline.

Invite to edit

Click on **Invite to edit** if you would like to collaborate with others in real time. When you click on **Invite to edit**, you will get a link for you to share with your collaborators. They will be able to access and edit your Prezi using this link. The page looks like the following screenshot:

Instant Prezi Starter

While collaborating, you will see avatars moving around the screen representing each collaborator. There can be up to 10 collaborators. The page looks like the following screenshot:

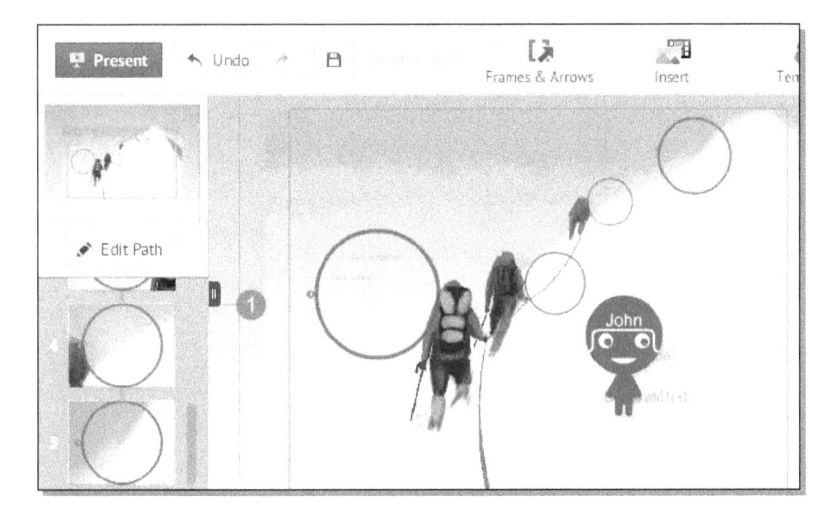

Start an online presentation

Click on the second item from the **Share** menu when you want to **Present online**. When you click on this button, you will get a link that you can send to your audience so that you can present in real time, and they will see the presentation on their screen even if they are in a separate geographic location from you. The page looks like the following screenshot:

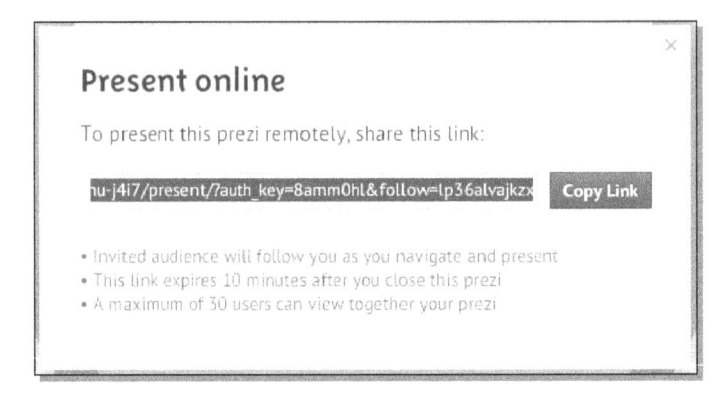

You have control of this presentation. This means your viewers will see what you want them to see. In this way, Prezi is ideal to use for presenting at a distance or during conference calls. You can send the link to your audience and present your Prezi while you're speaking through the phone or through the Internet in real time. They can zoom around and move forward or back, but once you click on a specific frame, it reverts back to the frame that you want them to see. While you're presenting, you will see how many guests are viewing your presentation at the same time. There will also be an indicator that you are the one presenting. You will see these indicators at the bottom of your presentation screen as shown in the following screenshot:

Download as PDF

If you want to have a hard copy of your Prezi project, you may want to save it in portable document format (PDF). To do so, click on the third item on the **Share** menu, **Download PDF**, as shown in the following screenshot:

Give it a few seconds to process, then select **Save PDF**. Make a note of the file name and location where you are saving your file so that you can find it. The page will look like the following screenshot:

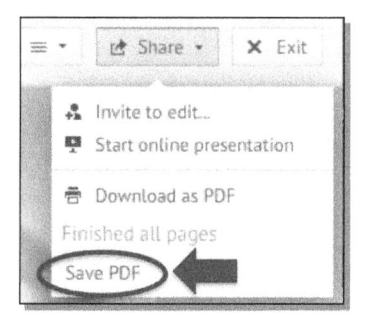

Post-editing options for your Prezi

There are many options for you to choose from once you're done editing your Prezi. Go back to your Prezi library and click on your first project. If you're in edit mode, click on the door button to exit. Take note of the buttons following the presentation: **Edit prezi**, **Present online**, **Download**, **Save a copy**, and **Share** as shown in the following screenshot:

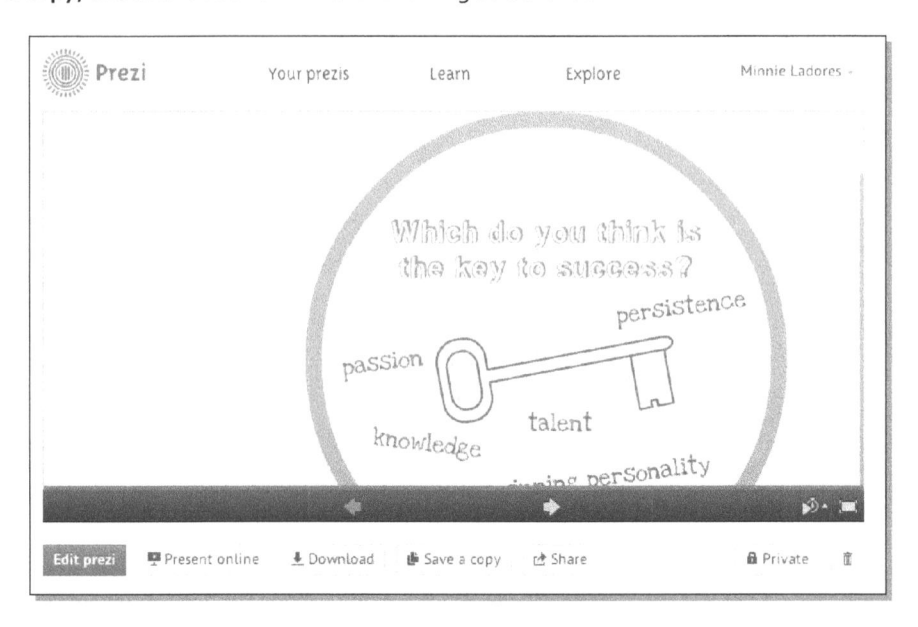

Edit Prezi

The first button is for editing your Prezi. When you click on **Edit Prezi**, the Prezi online editor is launched and you can make changes to your presentation.

Present online

Click on the second button when you want to present online. When you click on this button, you will get a link that you can send to your audience so you can present in real time and they will see the presentation on their screens.

Download

Sometimes, you may not be sure that you will have Internet access during your presentation. To make sure that you have a Prezi to present with, you may want to download a portable copy. You can either export to portable Prezi or download your presentation to Prezi Desktop (using Prezi Desktop is beyond the scope of this book) as shown in the following screenshot:

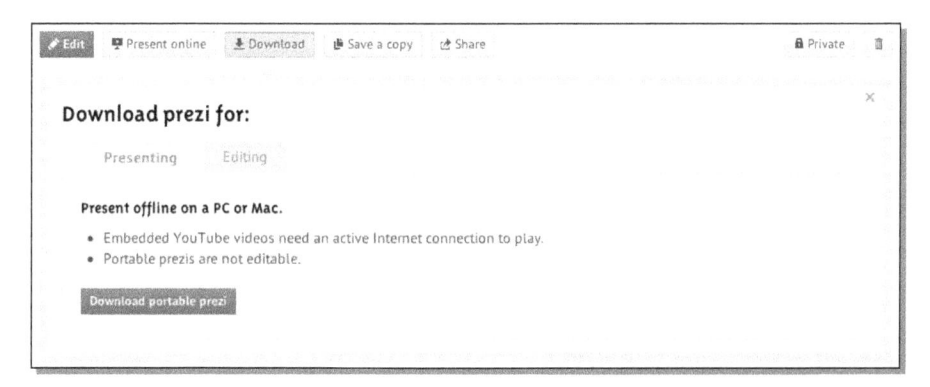

To present offline on a PC or Mac, click on **Download** then select the tab labeled **Presenting**. Click on the blue button, **Download portable prezi**. Give a few seconds for packaging your downloadable Prezi. The page will look like the following screenshot:

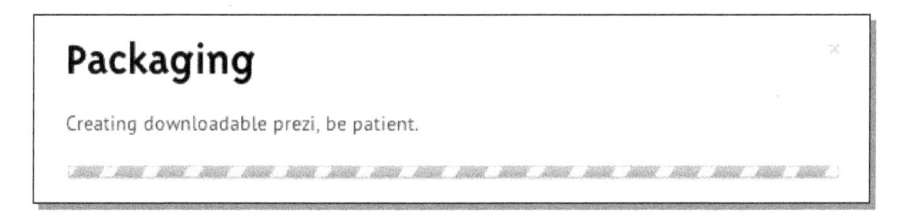

You will be informed when your Prezi is ready to be downloaded. Click on the link to download the file as shown in the following screenshot:

This action will create a folder within your desktop with a Prezi file. Click on the Prezi file to view your presentation offline. This is a portable Prezi. Portable Prezis will play offline. However, it cannot be edited. If there are embedded YouTube videos within a portable Prezi, these will not play unless there is an Internet connection.

Instant Prezi Starter

Save a copy

The fourth button is for saving a copy of your Prezi. This copy is saved online. You may opt to do this when you want to make changes on a presentation but you're not sure that you would like the changes. If you create a copy, then you're assured of having the original to revert back to in case the changes you made in the copy are not to your liking. The second file will have the words `Copy of` before the original title as shown in the following screenshot:

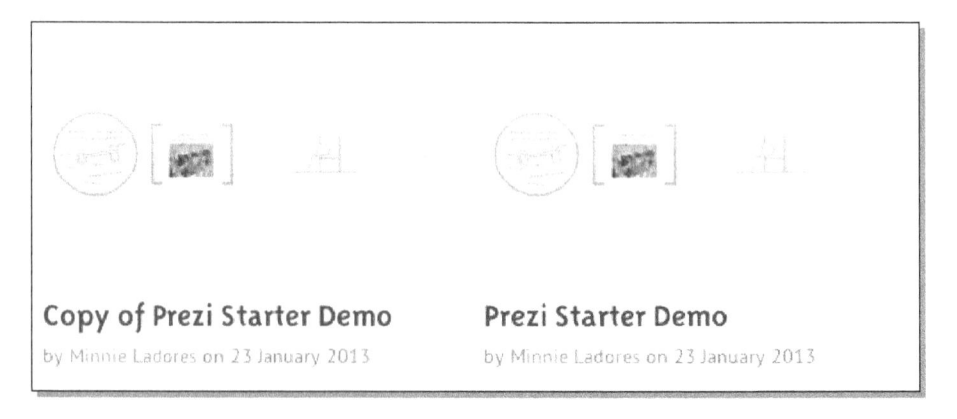

Share

You can invite others to view your Prezi asynchronously by clicking on the **Share** button and selecting the option for **Viewing**. When you select this option, you will get a web address that you can e-mail to your viewers. When your viewers click on this link, they will be able to see your Prezi presentation. They can move forward or back, or zoom in and out of this presentation in their own time (not real time or synchronous such as in a Prezi meeting). The page will look like the following screenshot:

There are times, however, that you might want to invite collaborators to edit a particular Prezi presentation along with you in real time. Click on **Share** and select **Editing**. Copy the link and send it to your collaborators. Or, click on **Email** and add e-mail addresses to send your Prezi to. Your collaborators will need to log in or sign up for Prezi in order to edit the document with you.

Sharing a Prezi is great not only for co-creating a presentation, but also for brainstorming in real time. Think of it as an online, virtual whiteboard on which your team can write notes and draw figures in real time while discussion is going on, whether face-to-face in a meeting room or collaborating through a telephone conference. Take advantage of the various templates and diagrams available on Prezi and use them for mind mapping ideas. Try it in your next company meeting.

Privacy settings

If you have a free Prezi account, all your work is automatically available to the public. If you have a Prezi Enjoy or a Prezi Pro account, your default setting will be private. People will not be able to see your presentation unless you have shared a link with them or you're presenting in person. To make your Prezi more accessible to others, change your privacy setting to **Public**. To do this, click on the button that says **Private** at the bottom of your presentation and select your preferred privacy state as shown in the following screenshot:

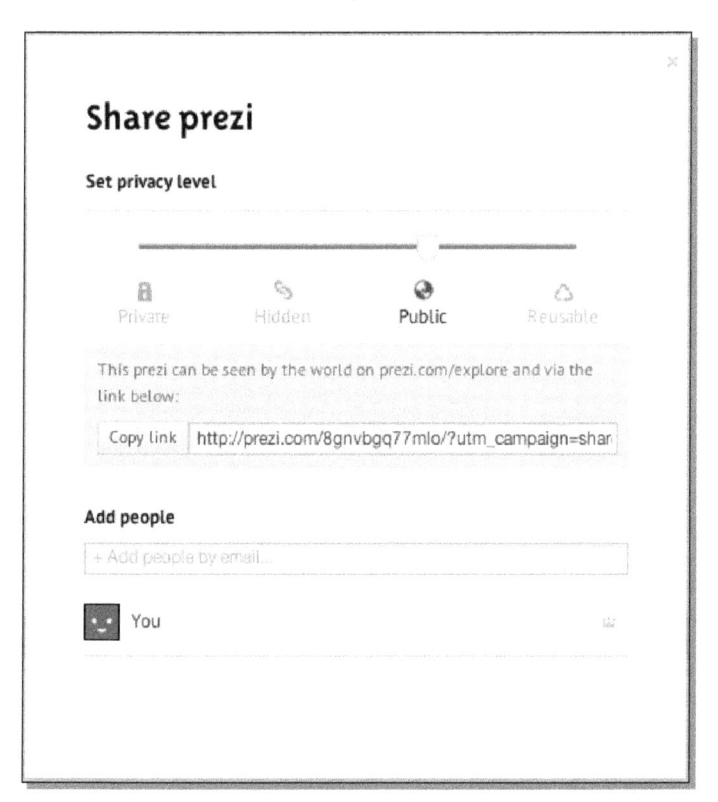

Deleting your Prezi

Finally, if you have created a Prezi that makes you cringe and you absolutely wish to get rid of it, don't you worry for a second! Just click on the trash can button next to the privacy setting button and your presentation will be gone. If you hit the trash can button by mistake, you'll have one chance to cancel. The page will look like the following screenshot:

People and places you should get to know

If you want to learn more about Prezi, following are links with useful information, inspiring ideas, and awesome examples:

Presentation tips

- Adam Somlai-Fischer, co-founder of Prezi, created this Welcome to Prezi presentation at `https://prezi.com/c1haylppbovo/welcome-to-prezi/`. A great introduction to Prezi in just one minute! Be sure to see Adam's other Prezis at `https://prezi.com/user/adam/`. Scroll down the screen to see his favorite Prezis created by other authors.

- A Presentation on Presentations by the Prezi Team: Watch and learn how to use Prezi tools to make your presentation have a great visual impact on your audience, including maximizing the use of metaphors and layout options at `https://prezi.com/mkg9y_p11cxd/presentation-on-presentations/`.

- Three Simple Steps to a Great Prezi: David Hooker wrote this short article with tips and tricks to help you get beyond the basics and to the next level. Go to `https://prezi.zendesk.com/entries/23449898-The-next-level`.

- Create a Prezumé! Take a look at resumés and portfolios created using Prezi then be inspired to create your own! Visit `http://prezi.com/explore/prezumes-and-portfolios/`.

Awesome Prezi examples

- 7 Outstanding Example Presentations Using Prezi, a blog posting by Angela Noble on The Daily Egg, available at `http://blog.crazyegg.com/2012/10/29/example-presentations-using-prezi/`.

- The Magical Theory of Relativity by the Prezi Team at `https://prezi.com/giwpfsdfpz0h/the-magical-theory-of-relativity/`.

- Typography by Travis Hitchcock – Check out this outstanding example of a Prezi at `https://prezi.com/ufnrer-swszq/typography/`.

- Get inspired by other people's projects at `https://prezi.com/explore/`. Search millions of Prezis from all over the world. Scroll down and take a look at ready-made Prezis that you can use.

Prezi company resources

- Would you like to see online demonstrations on how to create presentations using Prezi? Check out these video tutorials at `https://prezi.com/learn/`.

- If you want to get into the nitty-gritty details, or if you have questions on specific tools, be sure to check the Prezi manual at `https://prezi.zendesk.com/forums`.

- Learn the latest developments and stay posted with the Prezi Company Blog, Zoom into Prezi, at `http://blog.prezi.com/`.

Copyright concerns

It is everyone's responsibility to comply with all applicable copyright and trademark laws. When you create Prezis, be sure that the text, images, and videos you use are copyright compliant. Prezi has a copyright policy statement available at `http://prezi.com/copyright/`. To read more about the Copyright Law, go to `http://www.copyright.com/Services/copyrightoncampus/basics/law.html`.

Thank you for buying
Instant Prezi Starter

About Packt Publishing

Packt, pronounced 'packed', published its first book "*Mastering phpMyAdmin for Effective MySQL Management*" in April 2004 and subsequently continued to specialize in publishing highly focused books on specific technologies and solutions.

Our books and publications share the experiences of your fellow IT professionals in adapting and customizing today's systems, applications, and frameworks. Our solution based books give you the knowledge and power to customize the software and technologies you're using to get the job done. Packt books are more specific and less general than the IT books you have seen in the past. Our unique business model allows us to bring you more focused information, giving you more of what you need to know, and less of what you don't.

Packt is a modern, yet unique publishing company, which focuses on producing quality, cutting-edge books for communities of developers, administrators, and newbies alike. For more information, please visit our website: `www.packtpub.com`.

Writing for Packt

We welcome all inquiries from people who are interested in authoring. Book proposals should be sent to `author@packtpub.com`. If your book idea is still at an early stage and you would like to discuss it first before writing a formal book proposal, contact us; one of our commissioning editors will get in touch with you.

We're not just looking for published authors; if you have strong technical skills but no writing experience, our experienced editors can help you develop a writing career, or simply get some additional reward for your expertise.

[PACKT] PUBLISHING

Instant Prezi for Education How-to

ISBN: 978-1-78216-354-1   Paperback: 60 pages

A fast-paced, practical guide to creating impressive presentations for your students and colleagues

1. Learn something new in an Instant! A short, fast, focused guide delivering immediate results
2. Learn to create engaging presentations for your students and colleagues
3. Convert existing PowerPoints into Prezi presentations
4. Create interactive presentations from scratch by adding video, images, and PDFs

Mastering Prezi for Business Presentations

ISBN: 978-1-84969-302-8   Paperback: 258 pages

Engage your audience visually with stunning Prezi presentation designs and be the envy of your colleagues who use PowerPoint

1. Turns anyone already using Prezi into a master of both design and delivery
2. Illustrated throughout with easy to follow screen shots and some live Prezi examples to view online
3. Written by Russell Anderson-Williams, one of the fourteen experts hand-picked by Prezi

Please check www.PacktPub.com for information on our titles

[PACKT] PUBLISHING

Instant HTML5 Presentations How-to

ISBN: 978-1-78216-478-4　　　Paperback: 64 pages

Create beautiful and functional presentations using the reveal.js library, HTML5, and CSS3

1. Learn something new in an Instant! A short, fast, focused guide delivering immediate results
2. Create presentations using HTML5 and run them straight from your browser
3. Easily publish presentations on your website by using modern web technologies
4. Extend reveal.js with custom JavaScript code

Instant Wijmo Widgets How-to

ISBN: 978-1-78216-186-8　　　Paperback: 82 pages

Learn how to use Wijmo tools to spend up UI development and browser compatibility through practical recipes

1. Learn something new in an Instant! A short, fast, focused guide delivering immediate results
2. Make calendars, sliders, dynamic and animated charts quickly and easily
3. Create a live stream chart displaying real time data
4. Roll out customized themes via JQuery UI themerollers

Please check **www.PacktPub.com** for information on our titles

Lightning Source UK Ltd.
Milton Keynes UK
UKHW02f1059210618
324537UK00005B/372/P